100 DAYS HAPPIER

100 DAYS HAPPIER

DAILY INSPIRATION FOR LIFE-LONG HAPPINESS

DOMONIQUE BERTOLUCCI

hardie grant books

For Sophia and Tobias
Lara and Joshua
Isabelle
Mia, Noah and Stella
Elena and Daniel

~

If you want to learn about happiness,
spend time in the company of a child.

Preface

'Happiness depends upon ourselves.'

– ARISTOTLE

I'M OFTEN ASKED, 'What is the secret to happiness?'

Most people are looking for happiness in all the wrong places. They think it's something they can *achieve* or *acquire*; they'll be happy when they've done this or got that. They're looking to discover *the one thing* that will guarantee their happiness, so they can relax and enjoy the ride.

Many years ago, following what I call my quarter-life crisis, I made the decision to be happy. I stopped trying to be perfect, worrying what other people thought about me and let go of my need to be in control. I ended a relationship, changed career and made the commitment to being proactive about my pursuit of fulfilment.

I also changed the way I had thought about happiness up until that time. I learned that while I deserved to be happy, it wasn't something I could take for granted. I also had to do something about it.

It's been almost twenty years since I first made that empowering decision and if I've learned anything in that time, it's that you don't just choose to be happy *once*. Lasting happiness is something that you need to create, each and every day, through the simple choices that you make.

When I wrote *The Happiness Code: Ten keys to being the best you can be*, I wanted to explain to people the *how* of happiness: the principles you need to adopt to make happiness a way of life.

This book takes those principles and shows you how to apply them in your life by making small daily changes in the way you think and act, changes that will ultimately create a fundamental shift in the way you feel about *who you are* and *the life you are living*.

You could sit down and read this book from cover to cover, but if you really want to be happy, choose one page each day and put that idea into action. It doesn't matter if you do this in sequence or choose a random page each day. What matters is that you do it, and keep doing it, until the actions described become second nature to you.

What's the secret to happiness? You're holding it in your hands.

If you would like to learn more about unlocking the secret to lifelong happiness you can download a range of free resources, including *The Happiness Code Workbook*, from **domoniquebertolucci.com**.

You can download the 100 Days Happier app from your favourite app store and get daily inspiration delivered direct to your phone.

Happiness is a choice.
Choose to be happy and you will be.

Choose a happy life

When you wake up each morning, take a moment to think about the kind of life you want to have.

Consciously choose to have a happy life: one that is filled with love, laughter, good health and success.

Then begin your day focused on the things you can do to make this your reality.

*So many of life's eventualities
are beyond your control.
Work out what things you can
influence and come to a peaceful
acceptance of the rest.*

Don't waste your energy

Sometimes everything will go your way and on other days nothing at all seems to go right.

If you are having one of *those* days, instead of wasting your energy raging against something you can't control, take a deep breath and accept it.

That way, even though the moment may be ruined, your day won't have to be.

Accept the past,
dream of the future,
but live in the moment.

Focus on today

Some people waste their time thinking of what might have been. Others spend all their time thinking of what could be.

If you want to get the most out of your day, make sure that today is where you focus your energy and attention.

Your expectations determine
your experience.
Expect the best from life
and you will usually get it.

Have the right attitude

Start each day expecting nothing but good things to come your way.

Even though life may present you with all manner of ups and downs, having the right attitude will ensure your day will be a good one regardless of what you are given to work with.

*Believe in yourself, believe in your
dreams and believe in your right
to achieve your dreams.*

Be confident in your future

Before you start your day, take a minute to visualise your life as if your hopes and dreams were your reality.

Pay attention to how comfortable and natural it feels to be living this life. Then carry that feeling of quiet confidence about the future with you as you go about your day.

One of the most powerful questions
you can ask yourself is,
'How do I hold myself back?'
Once you know the answer
you can get out of your way.

Don't hold yourself back

Listen to your inner dialogue. Every time you find yourself saying 'but' to one of your ideas, what you are really doing is putting an obstacle in your path.

Challenge yourself today to rethink your ideas as if there were no 'buts'.

*Worrying about money is
one of the biggest causes of
unhappiness, but no amount
of money can make you happy
unless you change the
way you feel about it.*

Enjoy your wealth

No matter how much money you have, it won't make you happy if you're not already happy. And no matter how much you spend, you won't be able to buy happiness either.

Remind yourself that a 'poverty' mentality might not have a big impact on the amount of money you have in the bank in the future, but it can have a dramatic effect on your ability to appreciate the real wealth and abundance in your life today.

*Being generous is not just about
the decisions you make with
your wallet. Being generous
with your time and energy
is just as important.*

Spend your time wisely

When life gets busy it's easy to put off getting in touch with family or friends with the excuse that 'there are never enough hours in the day'.

If you find yourself holding back from connecting with someone you love today because you don't have the time, remind yourself that you do. You just need to make a better choice about how to spend it.

*Although happiness is a state
of being, it usually still requires
some doing if it is to be
lasting in your life.*

Make yourself happy

Ask yourself, 'What can I do today that will make me happy?'

This doesn't have to be a grand gesture or lofty goal. Just come up with one simple idea each day … and then go and do it!

Being the best you can be takes courage. You need to own your decisions and have the courage to see them through.

Make conscious decisions

It's easy to allow yourself to drift from one thing to another without ever really taking charge of your life. But not making a decision is actually a decision in itself.

If you find yourself considering your options today, be decisive. If you practise this on the little decisions, making bigger decisions will soon come more naturally to you too.

Perfectionism is a lost cause.
Focus your energy on being
the best you can be.

Simply do your best

Being perfect is an impossible goal.

Instead of pursuing perfection, make the commitment today to simply do your best. Then relax, confident in the knowledge that your best is always good enough.

Choose your battles wisely.
Unless you have a very high chance
of victory, spare your energy
and walk away.

Walk away

If someone annoys you today, regardless of whether the issue is big or small, ask yourself if it is a battle worth fighting.

Unless you are one hundred per cent sure of the answer, take a deep breath and walk away.

*Learning from the past
can help you move forward.
Lingering in the past
will only hold you back.*

Look for the lesson

At the end of each day, ask yourself, 'What did I learn?' and 'What would I do differently next time?'

Armed with your answers, you can leave the past firmly where it belongs and focus on making each new day your best one yet.

Worrying doesn't change anything.
Focus your energy
on the outcome you want
and then do what you can
to make it happen.

Take action

If you find yourself worrying about something today, stop.

Ask yourself, 'Is this something I can do something about?'

If you can't do anything about it, then worrying is a waste of your energy. If you can do something, put your energy to better use by taking action.

Your life paradigm is the set of beliefs or operating system for your life. Make sure you choose one that supports lifelong happiness.

Upgrade your thinking

If you find the same thing going wrong in your life over and over, take responsibility and ask yourself, 'What belief do I hold that is perpetuating this pattern?'

Make the commitment today to upgrade your operating system. Uncover your limiting beliefs, and embrace a set of thoughts and behaviours that support *you* in the life you want to create.

*Being happy
is not a privilege –
it is something
everyone deserves.*

You deserve to be happy

Remind yourself today that you really *are* worth it, that you *do* deserve to be happy and that it *is* your right to be happy.

Nothing is more powerful than the recognition that you deserve to be living the life you want.

*Just because there are things
you still want, that doesn't mean
you can't feel gratitude for all the
wealth and abundance
already in your life.*

Count your blessings

When you are focused on improving your life, it's easy to forget how fortunate you are.

Make the time each day to count your blessings. Chances are, your life is already rich in many ways.

If you are generous in your relationships you will receive as much as you give.

Don't keep score

Don't fall into the habit of keeping score in your friendships.

If a relationship is based on mutual respect and shared values, it doesn't matter who phoned whom last or whose turn it is to pay for coffee.

Make a point today of being the one to act first, not last.

*Commit to being happy
and make the choices that will
support your commitment.*

Make smart choices

Make the decision today to think before you act.

Every time you are faced with a choice, instead of just taking the easy way, ask yourself, 'What is going to make me happiest in the long term?' and go with that option instead.

*Live your life
with courageous integrity.
Do the right thing,
not the easy thing.*

Live with integrity

If you find yourself faced with a difficult decision today, don't just make the easy choice. Ask yourself, 'What is the right thing to do?'

As difficult as your answer may be, remind yourself that taking the easy way out will always be harder in the long run.

True happiness is a state of being,
not one of doing or having.

Breathe slowly and smile

One of the fastest ways to embrace a sense of happiness and wellbeing is to focus on the feeling you want to create.

Close your eyes, breathe slowly and smile. Keep smiling until you feel a sense of calm contentment wash over you.

Take a moment to capture how good that feels and then carry this feeling with you for the rest of your day.

Don't be attached to outcomes.
Enjoy your experiences for what
they are, what you have gained
and what you have learned.

Think about what you have learned

Instead of becoming disappointed or feeling let down if something doesn't turn out the way you wanted today, shift your perspective and ask yourself, 'What have I learned?'

When you are able to focus on what you've gained you'll be able to turn every experience into a positive one, regardless of the outcome.

Nobody from your past should be held responsible for your future. The only person accountable for your future is you.

Choose to have a great day

It's easy to fall into the habit of blaming other people for how your day turned out: the bus driver who was rude, the co-worker who was impatient, the guy who stole your parking space.

The truth is, nobody else has the power to make your day good or bad. It's up to you.

Make the decision that today is going to be a great day and don't let anyone else stand in your way.

Don't deny your emotions and force yourself to smile when you feel like crying. Cry, but learn to smile through your tears.

Embrace your feelings

In every full and interesting life there will be sad times as well as happy ones.

If something leaves you feeling low today, you don't need to deny yourself that feeling. Allow yourself to experience it fully; just remember not to wallow in it.

Your self-esteem is a valuable resource. Make sure you encourage, nurture, protect and support yours.

Treat yourself with respect

Constantly criticising yourself or using a harsh tone is not the way to get the best out of yourself.

Listen to your inner dialogue and make the commitment today to only ever speak to yourself with kindness, patience and love.

Your self-esteem is one of your most precious possessions. Treat yours with the respect it deserves.

You have to give yourself
permission to be happy.
Nobody else can give it to you.

Give yourself permission

If you find yourself making excuses or apologising for the things you want, stop. There is no reason why you can't have everything you need to create a happy and fulfilling life.

Give yourself permission today to do, be and have all that you want from life. Then go and make it your reality.

*Having a poverty mentality
leaves you focusing on all the
things you don't have, when in
reality you probably already have
everything you need.*

Decide to feel rich

If you spend your time thinking that you are poor, you will be. The truth is, even if there are things you still want for your life, you probably already have everything you need.

Every time you take out your wallet today, remind yourself how fortunate you are just to be able to do so.

Everyone has a different journey in life. Don't judge someone else for theirs.

Don't make judgements

Looking down at someone or thinking that you are better than them will never make you happy.

While feeling superior might give you a quick, short-term high, it will only last until you let that same judgement determine that someone else is better than you.

Make a commitment today not to judge. Even if the person you are judging is you.

Don't take your happiness for granted. Be proactive about maintaining and sustaining it in your life.

Be proactive

If something has been bothering you, wearing you down or getting on your nerves, don't just ignore it.

Make the commitment today to being proactive about your happiness and address whatever is getting in your way.

There is a big difference between being self-ist and being selfish – putting yourself first doesn't mean you have to put everyone else last.

Take care of yourself

Make a point of putting yourself first today.

While it might not be possible for you to be your number-one priority every single day, it's important to have your own needs met if you want to have the energy it takes to be there for everyone else.

You only have one life.
Make sure that yours is
one you are happy
to be living.

Do something just for you

As you work through all the things on your to-do list, make sure you find time for something just for you. It might be that you exercise, stop for a coffee at your favourite café, call a friend or read a chapter of a book.

Whatever you choose, make sure that you do something each day that you really do enjoy. Your life will be happier for it.

*Unless you have a crystal ball
you don't know how the
future is going to unfold.
Focus on the things you can
influence and don't fret
over the rest.*

Use your energy wisely

If you find yourself worrying today about things that haven't happened yet, stop. There really isn't any point.

Instead of fretting over things that may never eventuate, put your energy to good use and focus on making the things you *do* want to happen into your reality.

Look for the joy in each and every day. Just because it isn't immediately obvious, that doesn't mean it's not there.

Remember: it's good to be alive

Make a point of acknowledging something good or positive each and every day.

Rather than making this a bedtime activity, try doing it at two or three different times during your day.

It's so easy to be caught up in the hustle and bustle of life that if you don't stop and pay attention, you might not notice how good it is just to be alive.

*See the world as being
filled with positive potential.
Focus your attention on
your intention and make that
potential a reality in your life.*

Focus on what you want

Most people spend a lot of their time complaining about things they don't want or don't have, only to wonder why their life stays exactly the same.

If you want to live your best life, start each day by focusing your attention on your goals and dreams. Then apply your efforts to making these your reality.

Regardless of your upbringing or formative experiences, it is never too late to start believing in yourself.

Believe in yourself

Make the decision today to believe in yourself, your dreams and your right to achieve those dreams.

It doesn't matter if this isn't how you felt yesterday, or if you don't yet have the confidence to know you will feel that way tomorrow.

Just begin each day with this thought in mind and watch your self-belief grow.

There is nothing wrong with wanting more. There is no reason why you shouldn't get everything you want from life.

Go after the things you want

If you find yourself feeling guilty or telling yourself off for wanting to do, be or have more in your life, stop.

You can have anything you want in life if you are willing to work for it.

Don't waste energy today beating yourself up for wanting more. Put that energy to good use to make your dreams come true.

*When you understand
the difference between
'want' and 'need', you will
finally realise how
rich your life really is.*

Distinguish between your wants and needs

Most of the things we say we *need* are really just things we *want*.

There is nothing wrong with wanting everything that life can offer, as long as you don't allow it to stand in the way of your happiness.

If you find yourself saying 'I need …' today, ask yourself if you really do.

Before passing judgement
on someone's choices,
stop and look at the questions
they were trying to answer.

Understand the other point of view

Today, before you label someone else's decision as being right or wrong, remember this is just your perspective. Take a minute to understand where they are coming from.

It still might not be the right approach for you but you'll have a much clearer idea of why it was the best answer for them.

Most people are fine with 'fine'
and okay with 'okay'.
If you want to be the best you
can be, make sure you're not.

Don't be complacent

When you lead a busy life, it can be easy to get so caught up in the day-to-day that you forget about the bigger picture. If you are not careful, you can let weeks, months or even years can go by without stopping to focus on what you really want from life and what you need to do to make that your reality.

Make the time today to think about your goals, hopes and dreams and then do one thing that takes you closer to making them your reality.

*Sometimes being happy will
require some difficult conversations.
Some of those conversations
will be with yourself.*

Be firm but fair

Sometimes you need to give yourself a reality check.

If you need to give yourself a pep talk today, don't use it as an excuse to beat yourself up. Be firm, fair and focus on what you need to do to get back on track.

Focus on what matters.
Honour your values
and make decisions
that are aligned with them.

Do the things that matter

It is hard to live a happy life if you don't take time to think about what matters most to you.

Start each day by asking yourself, 'If I could do just one thing to make my life happy today, what would it be?'

Then make sure you do it.

*Let go of the idea of winning
or losing. In the game of life,
the most important thing
is just showing up
and doing your best.*

Aim for your personal best

Every time you evaluate yourself against someone else, you're competing. And every time you compete in this way, not only do you set yourself up for failure, you erode your self-esteem.

The only person you should ever compete against is yourself.

Make the commitment each day to aim for your personal best … Now that's a challenge worth meeting.

It's hard to be present
when your attention is suffering
information overload.
Switch off and just sit still.

Seek out silence

Find time to experience five minutes of silence in your day: walk away from your computer, put your phone on silent, close your eyes and just breathe.

Then return to whatever it is you need to focus on, feeling refreshed and re-energised. It will only take five minutes but you'll feel like you've been recharging for five hours.

Don't be afraid to take a chance.
The worst that can happen is that
you don't succeed ... this time.

Live without regret

Make the promise today to live without thinking 'If only … '.

The price you will pay for not being brave is a life of regret. The reward for being bold will be the satisfaction of knowing that you tried.

Examine your self-talk.
Never speak to yourself
more harshly than you would
to a small child.

Guard your self-esteem

Some of the most important conversations you have are the ones you have with yourself.

Pay attention to your inner dialogue today and make sure the things you tell yourself support, rather than erode, your self-belief and sense of self-worth.

You are the guardian of your self-esteem. Make the commitment each day to protect and nurture yours.

Challenge your assumptions
and identify your limiting beliefs.
Every time you find yourself thinking
that you can't do something,
ask yourself, 'Why not?'

Act as if it were true

Challenge yourself to suspend reality and spend the whole day acting 'as if … '. As if anything you wanted to do, be or have was possible.

As you view your world through this new perspective, you will begin to see the answers and solutions you need to make your dreams a reality.

*There is nothing wrong
with enjoying life's luxuries
as long as your happiness
isn't contingent on them.*

Find happiness within

There is nothing wrong with wanting nice things for yourself, if you want them for the right reasons.

If you catch yourself today thinking, 'I'll be happy when I've got this or I've done that', remind yourself that the things you've bought and the places you've been don't define your life, they're simply how you accessorise it.

Most people are doing their best,
most of the time.

Recognise the effort

If someone does something today that annoys or frustrates you, before you let it get to you remind yourself that they are probably doing the best they can.

Just because their best wasn't good enough for you, that doesn't mean they weren't making an effort.

*When you decide to be the best
you can be, don't be surprised
if the circle of people you
want to spend your time with
becomes smaller.*

Recognise your true friends

When you decide to be the best you can be, you might find it challenges the status quo in some of your relationships; not everyone wants to be reminded that their happiness is their own responsibility.

If you find your friendships are changing, make the decision today to accept it.

Your true friends will be happy for you and before long, those who aren't won't matter.

To be happy, you need to do
the right thing for you,
even when it feels like the
hardest thing in the world.

Do the right thing

Sometimes the hardest thing to do is the most important.

If you are faced with a challenging situation today, remind yourself to have courage and that your bravery will be rewarded in the long run.

When you make a choice,
acknowledge all the consequences.
That way you won't be left
feeling compromised.

Consider the whole picture

It's important to remember that no matter how good something sounds, everything has an upside and a flipside.

As you think about your options today, make sure you take some time to consider the downside as well as the up.

You can then make your decision confident in the knowledge that it's unlikely there will be any unpleasant surprises.

*No matter how much
you care about someone,
you can't take responsibility
for their happiness.*

Show them you care

Just as no one else is responsible for your happiness, you can't be responsible for someone else's happiness either.

If someone you care about is unhappy today, find a way to show them you care without taking on their problems as your own.

*Be there when you are there.
Don't try to juggle all the roles in
your life. Focus on the role you are
playing and do it to the best
of your ability.*

3rd

Don't try to juggle

Whenever you feel that you are juggling, you are really setting yourself up for guilt, frustration and a feeling of failure.

Make the commitment today to give the role that you are engaged in your complete attention for its duration. When it's time to swap roles, make the swap fully; don't leave half of yourself behind.

Remember, the thrill of watching a juggler in action is waiting to see if he will drop the ball.

Being optimistic isn't about believing nothing can go wrong. An optimist acknowledges what can go wrong but expects things to go right.

Plan for success

If you find yourself faced with a challenge or opportunity today and are unsure what to do, take a minute to ask yourself, 'How bad could it really get?'

Once you've considered the worst thing that could happen, you will be much better prepared to plan for the best.

*The happiest, most successful
people believe in themselves
unconditionally. They know
they can do, be and have all
that they want in life.*

Give yourself
the best chance

If you find that you are doubting yourself today, stop.

Unless you can see into the future, you can't know how things will turn out, but if you make the commitment to believing in yourself you will give yourself the best chance of success.

*So many people sabotage
their own chances for happiness.
Don't be one of them.*

Resist temptation

If you find yourself wanting to give in to temptation today, don't.

Remind yourself that your hopes, dreams and ideas are worth so much more to you than a few moments of instant gratification.

*Most of the things you
find yourself wanting
will have little or no bearing
on the happiness in your life.*

Be happy regardless

It's so easy to fall into the trap of thinking that getting certain things will make you happy.

Whether it's a promotion, a car or a bigger house, it's important to remember that nothing can make you happy if you are not already happy.

Make a commitment today to be happy regardless of what you have, not in spite of what you don't.

*If you want to be
the best you can be,
don't judge anyone.
Not even yourself.*

Don't criticise yourself

Don't be your own harshest critic.

Instead of judging yourself today based on whether you have failed or succeeded, evaluate your efforts and decide if you gave yourself a winning chance.

The only person who can take responsibility for your happiness is you.

Be happy with who you are

Start each day with the affirmation 'I am happy with who I am and the life I live'.

Begin each day with this simple thought and before long it will become your reality.

*It's easy to be brave when
everything is going your way.
When the going gets tough,
it takes courage to follow
the path you believe in.*

Get back on track

It takes courage to create your best life. It takes even more courage to stick to that goal when things are not going to plan.

If you are faced with a setback or disappointment today don't be tempted to quit. Instead, take a deep breath, dust yourself off and know that the only way forward is to get back on track.

There is no such thing
as 'no choice'. There are
always other options.
Explore yours.

Explore your options

Instead of making the obvious choice today, whether that's your coffee, your route to work or your favourite lunch, think about the other options available to you and choose something else.

Sometimes stepping out of your day-to-day comfort zone is all it takes to open your mind to the different options available in life.

*You can't make someone
do something just because
you want them to.
What you do have, however,
is the opportunity to
influence their choices.*

Look for the common ground

If you need someone to do something for you or to do it your way, think about what's in it for them.

Instead of seeing it as a battle of wills, if you are faced with a conflict today, view it as a chance to create a meeting of minds.

Multi-tasking is stressful.
You will get things done
much faster if you do them
one at a time.

 3rd

Do one thing at a time

One of the easiest things you can do to enhance the quality of your day is to try to do less.

Focus on doing one thing at a time and doing only that one thing until it's completed, regardless of what else you think you should be doing.

Remember, ten per cent of ten things isn't one hundred per cent of anything!

*Remember, however bad things
might be right now, this moment
will pass and your life will continue
to be a good one.*

Take a deep breath

Nothing lasts forever, not even the bad times.

If you find yourself having a tough day, take a deep breath and remind yourself that 'This too will pass'.

*Don't depend on others to
fuel your self-belief.
Develop your self-belief so that
it becomes self-sustaining.*

Know that you are good enough

Don't fall into the habit of looking to other people for validation or approval.

Remind yourself each day that you *are* good enough and that you don't need anyone else to tell you for it to be true.

It is only when your actions and words are aligned that you can achieve your true potential.

Walk your talk

It's easy to talk about what you want to do, be or have. It takes a lot more energy to take action.

Align your efforts with your intentions by making a commitment each day to do three things that will take you closer to your goal.

*Find a way to express your
gratitude for the wealth
and abundance in your life.*

Express your gratitude

At the end of each day, take a minute to express your gratitude for all that you have in your life.

It doesn't matter if you give thanks to God, the universe or even just yourself. All that matters is that you remember to say thank you.

*Remember to afford yourself
the same generosity
you give to others.*

Be kind to yourself

If something doesn't go your way today, don't beat yourself up.

Instead of chastising or criticising yourself, extend yourself the same kindness, encouragement and support that you would a good friend.

*If someone tries to undermine
your commitment, re-evaluate
your commitment to them.*

Carry on

When you have a goal you want to achieve, most people you know will be happy for you. Some people, however, may feel unhappy, uncomfortable or even threatened by the changes you are planning to make.

If it feels like someone is trying to undermine you or your efforts today, ignore them. Remind yourself that their behaviour is about them, not you, and carry on with your plans regardless.

Be honest with yourself.
You can't be the best
you can be unless you know
who you really are.

Don't make promises you can't keep

If you want to be the best you can be today, be honest with yourself about both your strengths and your not-so-strong points.

Don't make promises to yourself or others based on the person you wish you were – promises you have no real chance of keeping.

Own up to the person that you are and be the best version of that person you can be.

Self-pity never leads to happiness.
Remind yourself that the situation
may not be ideal, but it's rarely the
worst that could ever happen.

Don't give in to self-pity

If something doesn't go your way today, don't fall into the trap of saying, 'Why me?'

Instead of giving in to self-pity, take a minute to think about how much worse things could really be.

Although this may seem negative at first, you will soon notice a boost of positive energy when you realise that things are never as bad as they could be.

The best way to get what you want from a situation is to have clarity about the outcome you want to achieve.

Start with the end in mind

Before you get started today, take a moment to visualise how you would like the day to unfold. See yourself walking through every part of your day with comfort and ease.

Then open your eyes and get ready for the day you *really* want to have to begin.

Having a vision is great,
but don't be so focused on
your next goal that you forget
to enjoy your achievements.

Acknowledge
your progress

Take a minute to think of things in your life
that you have succeeded at or achieved, and
give yourself a pat on the back for making
these goals or dreams a reality.

Make time today to acknowledge all that
you have already achieved no matter how
long ago it was.

*Most of the things that go wrong
in life don't have a lasting impact.
Remind yourself that if it won't
matter in ten years time,
it doesn't matter today.*

Don't let it ruin your day

When something goes wrong it's easy to feel overwhelmed by the disappointment or frustration you are experiencing.

Although it might feel like it will have a lasting impact, in reality it probably won't.

If something goes wrong today, let the moment pass and don't let it ruin your whole day.

*When you believe in yourself
it is easier not to take
criticism, knock-backs and
disappointments personally.*

Don't doubt yourself

Unless you have asked for someone else's opinion, you don't have to accept it. And even if you did ask for it, it's up to you to decide whether or not you want to take the advice on board.

If someone gives you feedback or criticism today that you don't want or need, thank them politely and then have the confidence to file their advice – in the bin.

*Every time you say 'but' you are
giving yourself a get-out clause.*

Just do it

Make your mind up. Do you want to succeed today or do you just want to *try* to succeed?

With the right amount of commitment and effort, you can get anything you want from life. But if all you are willing to do is *try*, you will have failed before you start.

*Focusing on scarcity
will only create more
of the same.*

Feel abundant

Don't waste time focusing on the things you don't have; it will only make you miserable.

Instead of spending your time and energy thinking about what is missing, make the decision today to relax and enjoy the knowledge that while your life might not be perfect, it's already pretty good.

*Be generous with your
time and energy. The harder
it is to give, the more
the other person deserves it.*

Be patient

When you are trying to get a lot done it can be easy to become impatient with people who are not moving at the same pace as you.

While this might be acceptable in a work situation, it can undermine your relationships if you allow this approach to enter your home life.

Make a point today of being patient with the people you love.

Very few changes in life are achieved without effort and a commitment to making that effort.

Never give up

When you first start working towards something you want in life, it can be quite challenging to stick to your goals or plan.

If you feel like giving up today, remind yourself that it might not always be easy, but in time it will come to you with ease.

*Unless you have the
courage to say 'no' to
the things you don't want,
it's hard to say 'yes' to
the things that you do want.*

Be brave

If you find yourself being pulled in lots of different directions today, don't make the mistake of saying 'yes' to everything in an attempt to keep everyone happy.

Instead, say 'no' to as much as possible, and save your time and energy for the things that you know will make *you* happy.

*Don't sabotage your
chance for happiness.
Own up to the real choices
you are making.*

Think it through

Start each day by thinking about how you would like it to unfold.

Pre-empt the decisions you think you may be faced with and decide in advance what will be the best action for you to take.

*Being a control freak
is a sign of a vulnerable
self-esteem. The better
you feel about yourself
the less you need to control
everything around you.*

Learn to let go

Trying to stay in control of everything all of the time is exhausting.

Today, why not save your energy and boost your self-esteem by just letting go? Things might not turn out perfectly, but they will still be good enough.

Nobody's life is perfect.
Rather than wishing
for things you don't have,
make the most of the
things you do have.

Focus on what you have

In our materialistic world, it's easy to fall into the habit of constantly focusing on the things that you wish you had.

Every time you find yourself thinking 'I want' today, challenge yourself to replace that thought with 'I have', and acknowledge the things that are already yours.

*Be mindful of the
company you keep.
Don't let negative people
cloud your vision.*

Avoid negativity

Think about the people you will be spending time with today. In an ideal world you would avoid anyone who is likely to be negative.

Even if that's not possible, decide that today is going to be a good day and don't let anything anyone else says or does have an impact on your mood.

*When someone else doesn't believe
in you or your dreams, remember
it's about them, not you.*

Believe in your dreams

If you find that someone you are talking to today criticises your ideas or pricks your balloon in some way, don't let it deflate you.

Not everyone has the courage or confidence to live their best life, but don't let their lack of self-belief undermine yours.

*There is nothing wrong with
deciding that you don't want
something, but if you do want it,
go out and get it!*

Don't make excuses

There is a big difference between quitting and walking away.

If you feel like something you have been working towards is no longer aligned with your values or going to meet your needs, feel free to walk away.

But if all you are really feeling is that things are a little tough today, don't let that become your excuse to quit.

Sometimes you have to risk or give up some of your financial wealth to have a richer life.

Set yourself free

Don't allow attachment to money or wealth
hinder your choices or constrain your options.

If you find yourself thinking that there
is some part of your life you would like to
change if only you could afford to, remind
yourself today that money should buy you
freedom, not chain you to a life you don't
really want.

*Give the people you love the
best of yourself, not the worst.*

Show your love

It's easy to take the most important people in your life for granted, leaving them at the bottom of your to-do list.

At the end of your life, the people whom you've loved and who have loved you will prove to be one of your greatest sources of happiness.

Make the commitment today to give them the time they deserve.

*Identify your driving motivation
and you will have all the
encouragement you need.*

Motivate yourself

If you want to get something done today, don't think about all the reasons why you 'should' be doing it.

If you really want to motivate yourself, think about how great you're going to feel when it's done.

Don't rely on the opinions of others.
Only you will know what is
right for you.

Trust yourself

Instead of looking for feedback and approval from other people, learn to trust in your own judgement and intuition.

Deep down, you know the right answers to whatever it is you are facing. Today make a point of asking the right questions.

Choose to be happy.
It's the only sensible option.

Choose to be happy

Start each day with the simple mantra 'It's good to be alive'.

No matter what happens today, keep this simple but powerful message close to your heart and at to the top of your mind.

*The only thing you have total
control over is who you choose to be.
Be the best you can be.*

Decide who you want to be

Start each day with a very clear intention of the kind of person you want to be.

Decide where you want to spend your time, what you want to devote your energy to and how will you communicate with the people around you.

Then go out there and be that person.

*It's okay to aspire to a better life,
but don't let it stop you from
enjoying the life you already have.*

Enjoy the life you have

Take a few minutes today to picture your life through the eyes of a stranger. If someone who wasn't from your world discovered your life, what would they think?

Although there may be things you still want to achieve or aspire to, chances are the life you are living is already pretty good.

Perfection is impossible.
Expecting the best from yourself
isn't about trying to be perfect;
it's about striving to be
the best you can be.

Give yourself an 'A'

If you find yourself stressing over the little details today, trying to make things perfect, remind yourself that if you were in school, getting something eighty per cent right would still get you an 'A'.

It's okay to strive for an 'A+' but don't exhaust yourself trying to achieve a perfect score.

If you believe in yourself,
anything and everything is possible.

Let go of your limits

Make the decision today to believe in yourself – unconditionally.

Listen to your inner dialogue and banish any limiting beliefs or doubts that could prevent this from becoming your reality.

*Just because there is an obstacle
in your path, that doesn't mean
you have to get off the road.*

Overcome your obstacles

It won't always be easy to get what you want from life, but just because something doesn't come to you quickly, doesn't mean you need to give up.

If you find an obstacle in your path today, put your mind to it and find a way over, under or around it.

*The only way to get an
understanding of the true wealth
in your life is to acknowledge all the
things you have to be grateful for.*

Be grateful

Start your day by acknowledging the things in your life that you are truly grateful for.

Hold this sense of gratitude close to your heart and as your day unfolds, remind yourself that no matter what happens you really are fortunate.

*Recognise how much
you have to give.*

Be generous

When you have things pulling you in different directions, it's easy to become selfish in your perspective.

Instead of focusing on everything you want or need, focus your attention today on what you could do or give to someone else.

*The most important
commitment you will ever make
is to being the best you can be.*

Always do your best

When you wake up each morning, make a conscious decision to be the best you can be.

If you make this commitment before you do anything else, it will inform the rest of your actions for the day and guarantee that you give nothing less than your best.

*Be courageous in your
decision-making.
Stand by your choices
and never look back.*

Be fearless

Be fearless in your decision-making.

Unless you have a crystal ball, you can't know what the future holds. You can only make the best decision for you, right now, based on the things you know today.

The only wrong decision is indecision, so consider your options, make a choice and then make it work.

Acknowledgements

M Y FIRST THANKS, as always, go to my wonderful agent, Tara Wynne, at Curtis Brown, for her never-ending belief in my work, and to the team at Hardie Grant for once again being such a delight to work with.

To my assistant, Dani Magestro. Thank you for your invaluable support. My working life is so much easier now that I have you on my team.

To all my clients, past and present, the inspiring people who attend my workshops and those who buy my online programs: thank you for inviting me to be a part of your journey.

To my readers who connect with me on my Facebook page, thank you for taking the time to share your experiences. I am humbled every time I hear how my work has impacted your life.

To my dear friend Brooke Alexander, thank you for being the first person I share my ideas with. Without you to bounce my thoughts off, my brain would probably explode.

To family and dearest friends. You've seen your names here before and I hope you know how loved and cherished you are.

A never-ending thank you to my mum for so many things, but not in the least for proofreading every word I write and championing everything I do.

To my darling Sophia and precious Toby, thank you for filling my days with so much joy. And to Paul, for everything, always.

About the Author

Domonique Bertolucci is the author of *The Happiness Code: Ten keys to being the best you can be,* and is the closely guarded secret behind some of the country's most successful people.

Passionate about living your life on your own terms, Domonique has a client list that reads like a who's who of CEOs and corporate figures, award-winning entrepreneurs and celebrities, and her workshops are attended by people from all walks of life, from all around the world.

Since writing her first book, *Your Best Life,* in 2006, Domonique has become Australia's most popular life coach. More than ten million people have seen, read or heard her advice.

Domonique divides her time between Sydney and London. She lives with her husband and young family, and in her spare time can be found with her nose in a book, watching a movie, or keeping up the great Italian tradition of feeding the people that you love.

~

domoniquebertolucci.com
facebook.com/domoniquebertolucci
twitter.com/fromDomonique

This edition published in 2017 by Hardie Grant Books,
an imprint of Hardie Grant Publishing
First published in 2013

Hardie Grant Books (Melbourne)
Building 1, 658 Church Street
Richmond, Victoria 3121

Hardie Grant Books (London)
5th & 6th Floor
52–54 Southwark Street
London SE1 1UN

hardiegrantbooks.com

A Cataloguing-in-Publication entry is available from the catalogue
of the National Library of Australia at www.nla.gov.au

100 Days Happier: Daily inspiration for life-long happiness
978 1 74379 391 6

Cover design by Arielle Gamble
Typeset in Plantin Light 11/17pt by Cannon Typesetting

Printed in China by 1010 Printing International Limited